ADOBE PHOTOSHOP

FOR BEGINNERS 2023

TRANSFORM YOUR VISION INTO
REALITY WITH THE POWER OF
PHOTOSHOP

by

MARY LAMBERTH

COPYRIGHT

Printed in the United States of America

© 2023 by Mary Lamberth

New Age Publishing

USA | UK | CANADA

TABLE OF CONTENTS

COPYRIGHT i

TABLE OF CONTENTS ii

PART 1 → INTRODUCTION TO ADOBE PHOTOSHOP 1

WHAT IS ADOBE PHOTOSHOP? 1

THE BENEFITS OF USING ADOBE PHOTOSHOP 2

GETTING STARTED 3

PART 2 → CREATING AND SAVING YOUR FIRST
DOCUMENT 5

STARTING A NEW DOCUMENT 5

ADDING AN IMAGE TO YOUR NEW DOCUMENT 8

SAVING DOCUMENTS.. 9

PART 3 → WORKSPACE AND INTERFACE 11

UNDERSTANDING THE PHOTOSHOP INTERFACE.... 11

CUSTOMIZING THE WORKSPACE........................... 16

NAVIGATING AND ZOOMING IN PHOTOSHOP 20

WORKING WITH PANELS.. 22

USING THE LAYERS PANEL..................................... 24

PART 4 → BASIC TOOLS 29

MOVE TOOL 29

SELECTION TOOLS 30

CROP AND SLICE TOOLS 32

PAINTING AND RETOUCHING TOOLS 33

DRAWING AND TYPE TOOLS................................. 36

PART 5 → BASIC TECHNIQUES AND TIPS.................... 39

TRANSFORMING AND DISTORTING OBJECTS 39

UNDOING CHANGES 41

WORKING WITH FILTERS....................................... 42

USING ADJUSTMENT LAYERS 44

WORKING WITH MASKS... 47

WORKING WITH LAYERS AND BLENDING MODES .. 49

PART 6 → IMAGE EDITING 51

UNDERSTANDING IMAGE RESOLUTION AND SIZE .. 51

UNDERSTANDING COLOR MODES.......................... 53

COLOR CORRECTION 54

RETOUCHING AND REPAIRING IMAGES 57

CROPPING IMAGES 58

SHARPENING AND BLURRING IMAGES................... 59

ADDING TEXT AND GRAPHICS 62

REMOVING THE BACKGROUND OF AN IMAGE 63

PART 7 → FILE FORMATS AND OUTPUT...................... 66

UNDERSTANDING FILE FORMATS........................... 66

EXPORTING PHOTOSHOP FILES 68

PRINTING IMAGES.. 69

EXPORTING PHOTOSHOP FILES FOR OTHER
SOFTWARE.. 71

SHARING PHOTOSHOP FILES 72

PART 8 → ADVANCED TECHNIQUES AND TIPS........... 75

USING ACTIONS AND BATCH PROCESSING............. 75

WORKING WITH 3D OBJECTS 78

WORKING WITH VIDEO 79

CREATING ANIMATIONS 81

USING PLUGINS AND EXTENSIONS......................... 84

PART 9 → CONCLUSION... 86

TIPS FOR IMPROVING YOUR PHOTOSHOP SKILLS... 86

RESOURCES FOR FURTHER LEARNING.................... 88

EXERCISES 88

OTHER BOOKS.. 90

PART 1 → INTRODUCTION TO ADOBE PHOTOSHOP

This part introduces you to Adobe Photoshop. It also explains the benefits of using Photoshop and how to start using it.

WHAT IS ADOBE PHOTOSHOP?

Adobe Photoshop is a powerful image editing software developed by Adobe Inc. It is one of the most popular and widely used image editing applications by designers, photographers, and creative professionals.

Photoshop allows users to manipulate, enhance, and modify digital images and graphics using various tools and techniques. With Photoshop, you can adjust the color and tone of an image, retouch and repair photographs, create graphics, and add effects and text to images.

Photoshop is also known for its advanced features, such as support for layers, filters, masks, and other advanced tools. It is available on both Windows and Mac operating systems and used in a wide range of industries, including graphic design, advertising, publishing, and photography.

THE BENEFITS OF USING ADOBE PHOTOSHOP

There are many benefits to using Adobe Photoshop for image editing and graphic design, including:

1. Versatility: Adobe Photoshop can be used for various tasks, from simple photo retouching to complex graphic design projects.
2. Advanced features: Photoshop offers a wide range of advanced tools and features, such as layers, masks, and filters, that allow users to create complex and detailed images.
3. Integration: Adobe Photoshop can be easily integrated with other Adobe software, such as Illustrator and InDesign, allowing seamless workflows and collaboration.
4. Industry standard: Photoshop is considered the industry standard for image editing and graphic design, meaning that software proficiency is often required for many creative jobs.
5. Customization: Photoshop allows for a high degree of customization, including the ability to

create and save custom brushes, presets, and actions.

6. Plugins: Many third-party plugins and add-ons are available for Photoshop, which can extend the software's functionality and allow users to achieve even more advanced results.

7. Community support: As one of the most popular image editing software on the market, a large community of users and resources are available to help users learn and master Photoshop.

GETTING STARTED

Getting started with Adobe Photoshop can be overwhelming for beginners, but here are some steps to help you get started:

1. Install Photoshop: If you haven't already, you'll need to purchase and download Adobe Photoshop. You can get a subscription to Adobe Creative Cloud, which includes Photoshop and other Adobe software, or you can buy Photoshop as a standalone product.

2. Familiarize yourself with the interface: Take some time to explore the Photoshop interface,

including the menus, panels, and tools. You can customize the interface to suit your workflow and preferences.

3. Learn the basic tools and techniques: Start with the basic tools and techniques in Photoshop, such as the selection tools, brush tools, and layers.

4. Practice with sample files: Adobe provides sample files you can use to practice your skills and techniques. These files can be found in the "Samples" folder within the Photoshop application folder.

5. Take online courses or tutorials: Many online courses and tutorials are available for learning Photoshop, including free resources and paid courses. Take advantage of these resources to learn new techniques and improve your skills.

6. Experiment and have fun: Be bold and experiment with different tools and techniques in Photoshop. The more you practice and explore, the more comfortable you'll become with the software. And remember, Photoshop is a creative tool, so have fun and let your creativity run wild!

PART 2 → CREATING AND SAVING YOUR FIRST DOCUMENT

This topic covers the fundamental steps to create and save a new document in Adobe Photoshop, including adding an image to the canvas and selecting the appropriate settings for your project. Following these steps will give you a solid foundation to start working on your creative projects in Photoshop.

STARTING A NEW DOCUMENT

When you open Photoshop for the first time, you will encounter a window that gives you the option to create a new document, open an existing one or choose a recent document. *However, if you do not see these options, click on File > New to create a new document.*

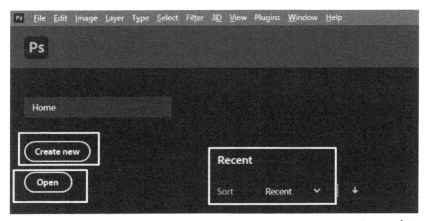

To create a new document, click "Create New", and a window will appear where you can customize your document settings. In this New Document dialog box, you can name your document, select its size, units, orientation, resolution, and color mode, and choose a preset size.

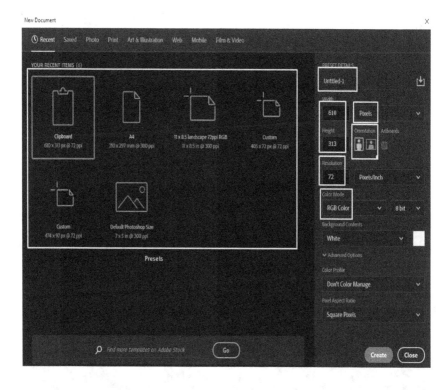

For beginners, it's recommended to name your document and change the measurement to inches, with a width of 12 and a height of 9. Set the orientation to landscape and the color mode to RGB, then click "Create" to confirm your settings.

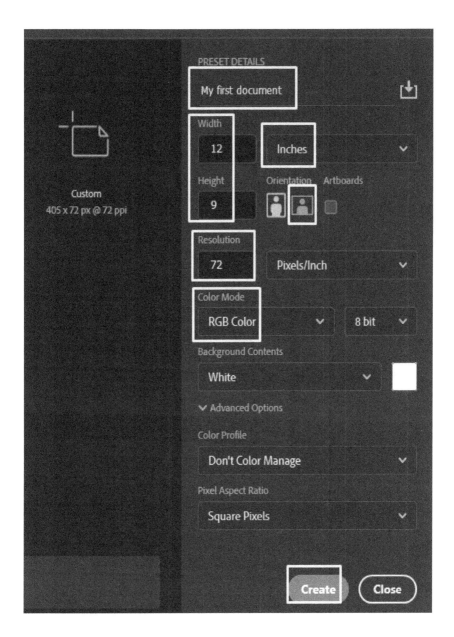

Once you have selected your settings, the Adobe Photoshop interface will open up, and you can start bringing your creative ideas to life.

ADDING AN IMAGE TO YOUR NEW DOCUMENT

It is easy to add an image to your document for editing. All you have to do is go to the menu bar and click File > Place Embedded to add an image to the document window. *You can practice with any image on your computer system.*

Click the "Commit transform" button or press the Enter key for Photoshop to accept the new image.

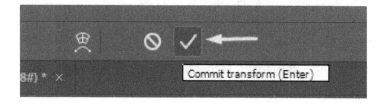

SAVING DOCUMENTS

Saving your work in Adobe Photoshop is a crucial step to ensure that you keep all progress and changes you have made to your design. Here's how to save a document in Adobe Photoshop:

1. Once you have completed your design or made changes to an existing document, click "File" in the top left corner of the screen.
2. Click on "Save" or "Save As" from the dropdown menu.
3. If you are saving the document for the first time, select "Save As." This will allow you to choose your document's file name and location.
4. In the "Save As" dialog box, choose the location where you want to save the document. You can also rename the document by typing a new name in the "File name" field.
5. Select the file format you want to save the document in. Photoshop allows you to save your document in several different formats, including PSD (Photoshop Document), JPEG, PNG, and TIFF. Choose the format that best suits your needs.
6. Click on the "Save" button to save your document. If you have made changes to an existing document, click "Save" to save the changes.

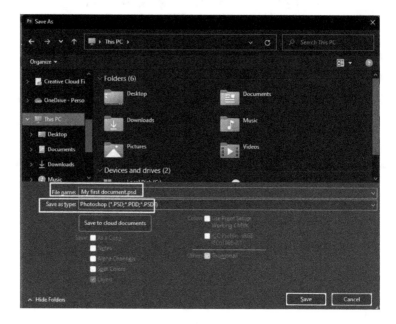

7. To quickly save a copy of your document, you can use the keyboard shortcut "Ctrl + Shift + S" on a PC or "Command + Shift + S" on a Mac. This will open the "Save As" dialog box and allow you to save a copy of your document with a new file name or in a different location.

Remember to save your work frequently, especially when working on large projects, to avoid losing any progress.

PART 3 → WORKSPACE AND INTERFACE

In Adobe Photoshop, a workspace refers to the arrangement of panels, menus, and toolbars within the application's interface. The workspace you choose determines the layout of the user interface and the displayed tools and panels. Adobe Photoshop provides several default workspaces, such as "Essentials" and "Photography", but you can also customize and save your workspace to suit your specific needs.

The interface in Adobe Photoshop is designed to provide easy access to the tools and settings needed to create and edit images. It includes various panels, menus, and toolbars that can be customized to create a personalized workspace. The panels in Photoshop provide access to functions such as layers, adjustments, and color, while the toolbars contain the tools needed to create and manipulate images. By customizing your workspace and interface, you can improve your productivity.

UNDERSTANDING THE PHOTOSHOP INTERFACE

The Photoshop interface can be intimidating for beginners, but understanding the different parts of the interface can help you navigate the software more efficiently.

Here are some of the key components of the Photoshop interface:

1. Menu bar: The menu bar is located at the top of the Photoshop window and contains various menus that allow you to access different features and options within the software.

2. Tools panel: The tools panel is located on the left side of the interface and contains a wide range of tools you can use to create and manipulate images. Some of the most commonly used tools

include the Move, Marquee, Lasso, and Brush tools.

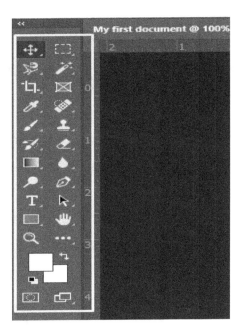

You can display other tools in a tool by clicking and holding a particular tool till others appear.

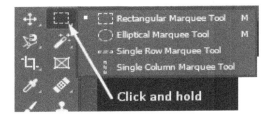

3. Options bar: The options bar is located just below the menu bar and displays options for the currently selected tool. For example, if you have the Brush tool selected, the options bar will

display options for the Brush tool, such as brush size, opacity, and hardness.

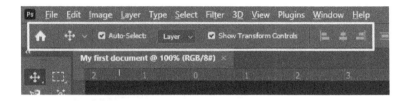

4. Panels: Panels are located on the right side of the interface and contain various tools and settings that you can use to customize your workspace. Many different panels are available in Photoshop, including the Layers panel, Color panel, and History panel.

5. Document window: The document window is where your image or project is displayed. You can have multiple documents open at once, and each document is displayed in its separate window.

6. Status bar: The status bar is located at the bottom of the interface and displays information about the current document, such as its size and resolution.

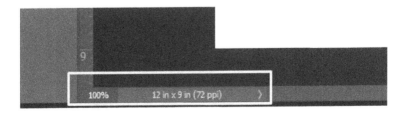

By familiarizing yourself with these different parts of the interface, you can easily navigate Photoshop and access the tools and features you need to create and edit your images.

CUSTOMIZING THE WORKSPACE

Customizing the workspace in Adobe Photoshop can help you work more efficiently and comfortably. Here are some ways to customize the workspace:

1. Rearrange panels: You can rearrange the panels in Photoshop by dragging them to different locations on the screen. You can also group related panels together by dragging them onto the same panel group.

2. Hide or show panels: You can hide or show panels by clicking on the panel's icon in the top right corner of the panel. This will toggle the visibility of the panel on and off.

3. Customize toolbar: You can change the look of the toolbar by clicking on the icon in the top left corner of the toolbar.

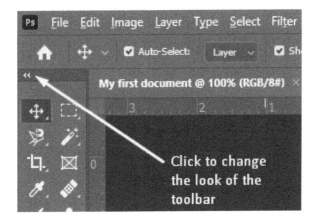

Click to change the look of the toolbar

4. Save workspace: Once you have customized your workspace, you can save it as a new workspace by going to the "Window" menu and selecting "Workspace" > "New Workspace". This will allow

you to save your customized workspace settings and access them later.

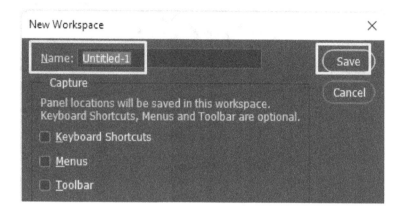

5. Load workspace: To load a saved workspace, go to the "Window" menu and select "Workspace". Select the workspace you want to load from the list of available workspaces.

6. Reset workspace: If you want to reset your workspace to the default settings, go to the "Window" menu and select "Workspace" > "Reset [Workspace Name]". This will reset your workspace to the default settings for that workspace.

7. Keyboard shortcuts: You can customize keyboard shortcuts in Photoshop by going to the "Edit" menu and selecting "Keyboard Shortcuts". This will allow you to customize existing keyboard shortcuts or create new ones.

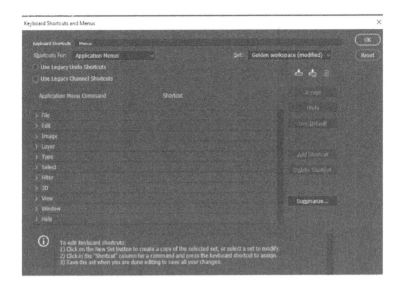

8. Color scheme: You can customize the color scheme in Photoshop by going to the "Edit" menu and selecting "Preferences" > "Interface". This will allow you to choose a different color scheme for the Photoshop interface.

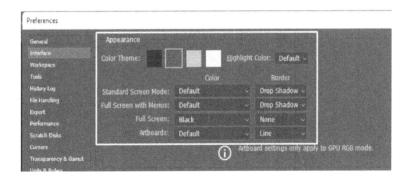

By customizing your workspace in Photoshop, you can create a more efficient and comfortable environment for working with images and graphics.

NAVIGATING AND ZOOMING IN PHOTOSHOP

Navigating and zooming in Photoshop is essential for working with images and graphics. Here are some ways to navigate and zoom in Photoshop:

1. Hand tool: The Hand tool allows you to move around an image larger than the document window. You can select the Hand tool by pressing the spacebar key on your keyboard or by selecting it from the toolbar.

Hand tool (H)

Pans over different parts of an image

Learn how

2. Zoom tool: The Zoom tool allows you to zoom in or out of an image. You can select the Zoom tool by pressing the Z key or by selecting it from the

toolbar. Clicking on an area of the image with the Zoom tool will zoom in, while holding down the Alt key (Option key on Mac) and clicking with the Zoom tool will zoom out.

3. Navigator panel: The Navigator panel allows you to zoom and navigate an image by clicking and dragging a rectangle around the area you want to view. You can access the Navigator panel by going to the "Window" menu and selecting "Navigator".

4. Zoom percentage: You can change the zoom percentage of the image by going to the bottom left corner of the document window and selecting the zoom level from the dropdown menu.

5. Keyboard shortcuts: You can use keyboard shortcuts to zoom in and out of an image. Pressing Ctrl + "+" (Command + "+" on Mac) will zoom in, while pressing Ctrl + "-" (Command + "-" on Mac) will zoom out.

Using these navigation and zooming techniques, you can quickly move around and view your images and graphics in Photoshop.

WORKING WITH PANELS

Working with panels and toolbars in Adobe Photoshop is essential for accessing the various tools and settings needed to create and edit images. Here are some tips for working with panels and toolbars:

1. Docking and undocking panels: Panels can be docked, or grouped, to save space in the workspace. You can undock a panel by clicking and dragging it away from the docked panels. To

dock a panel, drag it to the edge of an existing docked panel until you see a blue line appear.

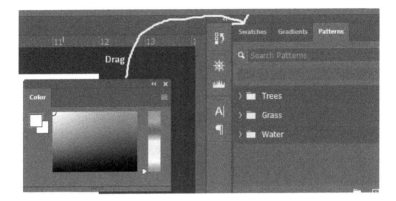

2. Resizing panels: You can resize a panel by clicking and dragging its edge or corner. This can be useful if you need to view more or less of the panel's contents.

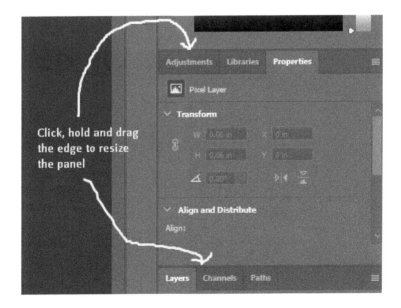

3. Collapsing and expanding panels: Panels can be collapsed or expanded by clicking the double-arrow icon in the panel's top right corner. This can be useful if you only need to access the panel occasionally and want to save space in the workspace.

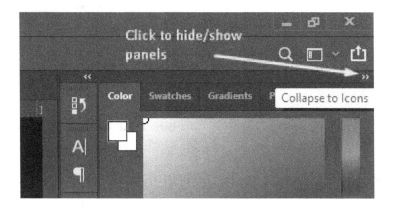

Using these tips for working with panels and toolbars in Photoshop, you can create a customized workspace that maximizes your productivity and efficiency.

USING THE LAYERS PANEL

The Layers panel in Adobe Photoshop is an essential tool for working with images and graphics. It allows you to organize and edit different elements of an image on separate layers. The Layers panel is located on the right side of the interface, and you can also access it through Window > Layers.

Here are some ways to use the Layers panel:

1. Creating layers: You can create a new layer by clicking the "Create a new layer" button at the bottom of the Layers panel or by going to the "Layer" menu and selecting "New" > "Layer".

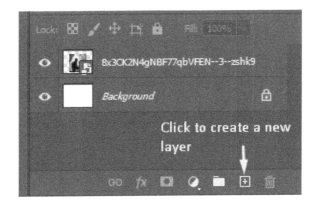

2. Renaming layers: You can rename a layer by double-clicking on its name in the Layers panel and typing a new name.

3. Rearranging layers: You can rearrange the order of layers by dragging them up or down in the Layers panel. The order of layers determines which elements are displayed on top of each other in the image.

4. Locking/Unlocking layers: You can lock a layer by selecting the layer and clicking the lock icon in the Layers panel. This will prevent you from accidentally making changes to the layer.

When you open a new document, a background layer is created for you, which is locked by default.

Also, you can unlock any layer by clicking the unlock button next to the layer.

5. Grouping layers: You can group layers by selecting the layers and then clicking the "Create a new group" button at the bottom of the Layers panel. This is useful for organizing elements of an image that are related to each other.

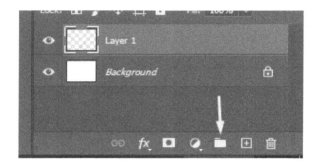

6. Blending modes: You can change the blending mode of a layer by selecting the layer and then choosing a blending mode from the dropdown menu at the top of the Layers panel. Blending modes control how the layer interacts with the layers below it.

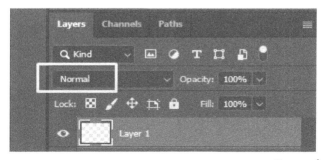

7. Opacity: You can adjust the opacity of a layer by selecting the layer and then dragging the opacity slider in the Layers panel. This controls the transparency of the layer.

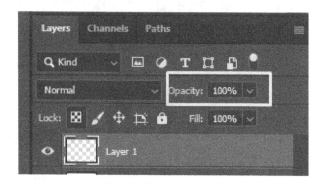

By using the Layers panel in Photoshop, you can organize and manipulate different elements of an image on separate layers, allowing for more efficient and precise editing. As we proceed, we will be making use of this panel.

PART 4 → BASIC TOOLS

This topic covers the various tools in Adobe Photoshop for basic image editing. Learning and mastering these tools and techniques can enhance your creativity and improve the quality of your digital designs and images.

MOVE TOOL

The move tool is represented by a pointer with four arrows icon in the toolbar, and it allows you to select and move layers, selections, and other objects within your design.

Here's how you can use the move tool in selecting objects in Photoshop:

1. Select the move tool from the toolbar on the left-hand side of the screen. You can also use the keyboard shortcut "V" to activate the move tool.
2. Click on the layer or selection you want to move. You should see a bounding box around the object, indicating that it has been selected.

3. Click and drag the object to move it around on the canvas.

4. If you need to nudge the object slightly to the left, right, up, or down, you can use the arrow keys on your keyboard while the object is selected. This can help make minor adjustments to your design.

5. You can also use the move tool to copy an object. To do this, hold down the Alt key on your keyboard (Option key on a Mac) and click and drag the object to a new location. This will create a copy of the object that you can move independently of the original.

6. To deselect an object, click anywhere on the canvas outside of the object.

SELECTION TOOLS

Selection tools are an essential part of Adobe Photoshop, allowing you to select specific areas of an image for editing or manipulation.

Here are some commonly used selection tools you can explore:

1. Marquee tool: The Marquee tool is used to create rectangular or elliptical selections. It's great for

selecting regular shapes or creating simple borders. *Click and hold the Rectangular Marquee tool to display other Marquee tools.*

2. Lasso tool: The Lasso tool allows you to make freehand selections around an object. It's great for selecting irregular shapes or objects with a complex outline. *Click and hold the Magnetic Lasso tool to display other Lasso tools.*

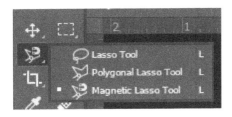

3. Magic Wand tool: The Magic Wand tool selects areas of similar colors with a single click. It helps select large areas of the same color or create selections based on contrast.

4. Quick Selection tool: The Quick Selection tool automatically selects areas of an image that are similar in color and texture. It's useful for selecting objects or people in an image quickly.

Using these selection tools, you can create precise selections that allow you to edit or manipulate specific areas of an image in Adobe Photoshop.

CROP AND SLICE TOOLS

The Crop and Slice tools are essential tools that allow you to adjust the size and composition of your images.

The Crop tool allows you to remove unwanted areas from an image and adjust the aspect ratio or size. To use the Crop tool, select the Crop tool from the toolbar or press "C" on your keyboard. Then, drag the Crop tool over the area you want to keep, and press Enter or Return to apply the crop.

The Slice tool, on the other hand, is used to divide an image into smaller sections, which can then be exported or saved separately. To use the Slice tool, select the Slice tool from the toolbar or press "K" on your keyboard. Then, click and drag over the area you want to slice, and release the mouse button. You can then adjust the slice properties in the options bar.

Both the Crop and Slice tools help optimize images for web or print. Using the Crop tool, you can ensure that your images are composed the way you want, while the Slice tool can be used to create web graphics with multiple parts.

In summary, the Crop and Slice tools are tools for adjusting the size and composition of your images and can be used for optimizing images for the web or print.

PAINTING AND RETOUCHING TOOLS

Painting and retouching tools in Adobe Photoshop are designed to help you create and edit images with precision and detail.

Painting tools allow you to add color, texture, and other visual elements to your images. They include the Brush, Pencil, Eraser, and Paint Bucket tools.

The Brush tool is one of the most commonly used painting tools, and it allows you to add color and texture to your images with various brush sizes, shapes, and opacities. The Pencil tool is similar to the Brush tool but creates a harder-edged line, while the Eraser tool allows you to remove parts of an image. The Paint Bucket tool fills a selection or layer with a solid color or gradient.

Retouching tools are used to edit and enhance images by removing imperfections, adjusting color and tone, and adding effects. They include the Healing Brush, Clone Stamp, Spot Healing Brush, and Dodge and Burn tools.

The Healing Brush and Spot Healing Brush tools allow you to remove unwanted objects, blemishes, or wrinkles from an image. The Clone Stamp tool is similar to the Healing Brush tool but will enable you to clone or copy an area of the image onto another area. The Dodge and Burn tools are used to adjust the brightness and contrast of specific parts of an image.

Overall, painting and retouching tools in Adobe Photoshop are essential for creating and editing images with precision and detail. By mastering these tools, you can add color, texture, and effects to your images, remove imperfections and enhance the overall quality of your work.

DRAWING AND TYPE TOOLS

Drawing and type tools in Adobe Photoshop are essential for creating vector-based graphics and text-based designs.

Drawing tools include the Pen, Line, Shape, and Custom Shape tools.

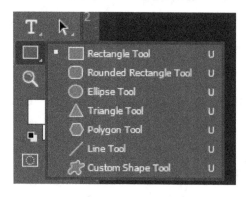

The Pen tool allows you to create precise paths and shapes that can be filled with color or used as a mask. The Line tool is used to draw straight lines, while the Shape and Custom Shape tools are used to create basic geometric shapes, such as squares, circles, and polygons.

Type tools allow you to add and manipulate text in your designs. They include the Horizontal Type and Vertical Type tools, enabling you to add text horizontally or vertically. You can also use the Type Mask tool to create a selection in the shape of the text, which can then be filled with color or used as a mask.

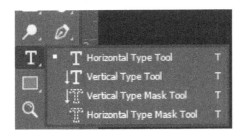

In addition to drawing and type tools, Adobe Photoshop offers various layer styles and effects that can be applied to your designs. These include Drop Shadow, Bevel and Emboss, and Gradient Overlay, among others.

Overall, drawing and type tools in Adobe Photoshop are essential for creating vector-based graphics and text-based designs. By mastering these tools, you can create precise and professional-looking designs that can be used for various purposes, such as logos, illustrations, and posters.

PART 5 → BASIC TECHNIQUES AND TIPS

Basic Techniques and Tips in Adobe Photoshop can help you improve your workflow, productivity, and creativity.

TRANSFORMING AND DISTORTING OBJECTS

Transforming and Distorting objects in Adobe Photoshop allows you to resize, rotate, skew, distort and warp your images and graphics to achieve your desired composition. Using these tools effectively will enable you to create more dynamic and visually appealing designs for your projects.

Here are the steps to Transform and Distort objects in Adobe Photoshop:

1. Select the object or layer you want to transform by clicking on it in the Layers panel.
2. Go to Edit > Transform to access the transformation tools.
3. Select one of the transformation tools, such as Scale, Rotate, Skew, Distort or Warp.
4. Use the transformation handles to adjust the object. Click and drag the handles to resize, rotate, skew, or warp the object.

5. Use the Options bar to adjust the transformation settings. For example, you can specify the degree of rotation or the amount of distortion.
6. Press Enter or click the checkmark in the Options bar to apply the transformation.

Note that you can also use the Free Transform command (Ctrl/Cmd + T) to access all transformation tools at once.

UNDOING CHANGES

Undoing changes in Adobe Photoshop is a helpful feature that allows you to reverse any edits or modifications made to an image. It enables you to go back in your editing history to a specific point in time, helping you correct any mistakes or experiment with different effects without worrying about making irreversible changes.

To undo changes in Photoshop, you can use the "Undo" command by pressing "Ctrl + Z" on a Windows PC or "Command + Z" on a Mac. You can also go to "Edit" in the menu bar and select "Undo" or "Step Backward" to undo multiple changes. Another option is to use the History panel to go back to a specific step in your editing process.

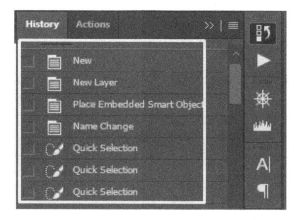

WORKING WITH FILTERS

Working with Filters in Adobe Photoshop allows you to apply various effects and adjustments to your images, such as blurring, sharpening, distortion, stylization, and more. Filters can help you achieve different looks and moods for your projects and save you time and effort in manual editing.

Here are the steps to use Filters in Adobe Photoshop:

1. Open an image in Photoshop that you want to apply a filter to.
2. Ensure the layer you want to apply the filter to is selected in the Layers panel.
3. Go to Filter in the top menu and select the type of filter you want to apply.
4. Choose the specific filter from the dropdown menu.
5. Adjust the filter settings in the dialog box that appears. The settings will vary depending on the type of filter you chose.
6. Preview the changes in the image window.
7. Click OK to apply the filter to the image.
8. If desired, you can further adjust the filter settings by going to Filter > Filter Gallery. This will open a dialog box with a range of filter options and settings.

Note that you can also apply filters to selected areas of an image using layer masks, adjustment layers, or other selection tools. Additionally, you can combine multiple filters and adjust their blending modes and opacity to create more complex effects. By experimenting with different filters and settings, you can enhance the visual impact of your images and bring your creative vision to life.

USING ADJUSTMENT LAYERS

Using Adjustment Layers in Adobe Photoshop allows you to make non-destructive changes to the color, tone, and contrast of your images. Adjustment Layers are separate layers that apply adjustments to the layers beneath them, without altering the original pixel data. This gives you more flexibility and control over your editing and enables you to make precise and reversible changes to your images.

Here are the steps to use Adjustment Layers in Adobe Photoshop:

1. Open an image in Photoshop that you want to adjust.
2. Click on the Adjustment Layers button at the bottom of the Layers panel.

3. Choose the type of adjustment you want to make, such as Brightness/Contrast, Levels, Curves, Hue/Saturation, Color Balance, or Black & White.

4. Adjust the settings for the selected adjustment layer in the Properties panel. You can use sliders, input fields, or eyedropper tools to adjust your image's color, tone, and contrast.

5. If you want to apply the adjustment to a specific layer or group of layers, drag the adjustment layer above the layer you want to apply it to.

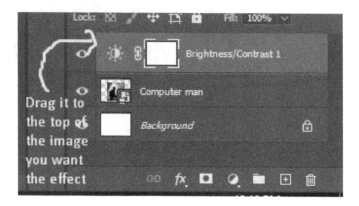

6. If you want to limit the adjustment to a specific area of the image, create a layer mask and use a brush or selection tool to paint or erase the mask.
7. If you want to make further adjustments to the same area or adjustment, you can duplicate the adjustment layer and modify its settings.
8. If you want to turn off or modify the adjustment layer later, you can simply click on the layer and adjust the settings in the Properties panel.

Note that you can also use Adjustment Layers in combination with blend modes, opacity, and layer masks to create more complex and subtle effects. By using Adjustment Layers, you can make global or local adjustments to your images without damaging the original pixel data and achieve a more professional and creative look for your projects.

WORKING WITH MASKS

Working with Masks in Adobe Photoshop allows you to selectively hide or reveal parts of an image or layer and create complex composites and effects. Masks are grayscale images that define the transparency of a layer, channel, or selection. Masks can be created, edited, and combined in various ways, and enable you to refine the edges, adjust the tones, or apply special effects to your images.

Here are the steps to work with Masks in Adobe Photoshop:

1. Open an image in Photoshop that you want to apply a mask to.
2. Select the layer you want to mask in the Layers panel.
3. Click on the Add Layer Mask button at the bottom of the Layers panel.

4. Use a Brush tool to paint on the mask with black, white, or shades of gray. Black hides the layer, white reveals the layer, and gray partially reveals the layer. You can adjust the brush's opacity, size, hardness, and flow to control the mask.
5. If you want to refine the edges of the mask, you can use the Refine Mask option in the Properties panel. This allows you to smooth, feather, contract, or expand the mask.
6. If you want to create a more precise or complex mask, you can use selection tools, such as Quick Selection, Magic Wand, or Lasso, to create a selection first and then convert the selection to a mask by clicking on the Add Layer Mask button.
7. If you want to combine or apply multiple masks to a layer, you can use the Mask panel or the Channels panel. This allows you to adjust the individual masks or channels and create intricate composites or effects.
8. If you want to disable or enable the mask temporarily, you can hold down the Alt key and click on the mask thumbnail in the Layers panel.

Note that masks are non-destructive and editable, meaning you can modify or remove them at any time. By working with masks, you can create precise and sophisticated selections, composites, and effects and achieve a more professional and creative look for your images.

WORKING WITH LAYERS AND BLENDING MODES

Working with layers and blending modes is a key aspect of Photoshop editing. Layers allow you to separate elements of your design or composition and work on them individually, while blending modes determine how the layers interact with each other. Here's an overview of how to work with layers and blending modes in Photoshop:

1. Create a new layer by clicking on the "New Layer" icon in the Layers panel or by pressing Ctrl+Shift+N (Windows) or Command+Shift+N (Mac).
2. Rename the layer to help you keep track of what it contains.
3. Use the tools and techniques in Photoshop to add content to the layer.
4. Adjust the opacity and/or blending mode of the layer to change how it interacts with the layers beneath it.

5. Experiment with different blending modes to achieve the desired effect. For example, the "Overlay" blending mode can create a subtle, dramatic effect, while the "Multiply" blending mode can create a darker, more contrasted look.
6. Use layer masks to hide or reveal parts of a layer. This can be useful for creating complex effects or for blending multiple layers together seamlessly.
7. Organize your layers by grouping them and naming them according to their contents.
8. Save your work by going to File > Save As and choosing a file format and location.

By using layers and blending modes in Photoshop, you can create complex, multi-layered designs and compositions with a high level of control and flexibility. With practice and experimentation, you can develop your skills and create stunning images and graphics.

PART 6 → IMAGE EDITING

Image Editing is a crucial aspect of Adobe Photoshop, and it allows you to transform, manipulate, and enhance your images in numerous ways.

UNDERSTANDING IMAGE RESOLUTION AND SIZE

Image resolution and size are important concepts to understand when working with images in Adobe Photoshop.

Resolution refers to the number of pixels in an image, and it is measured in pixels per inch (PPI) or dots per inch (DPI). The higher the resolution, the more detail and clarity the image will have. However, higher resolution also means larger file sizes, which can impact the performance and storage of your computer.

Image size refers to the physical dimensions of an image, such as width and height, and it is measured in inches, centimeters, or pixels. The size of an image can affect its appearance, especially when printed or displayed on different devices or media.

When working with images in Photoshop, you can adjust the resolution and size of an image using the Image Size dialog box by going to Image > Image Size.

Here are some tips to keep in mind:

- To change the resolution of an image without affecting its physical size, uncheck the "Resample" option and change the value of the resolution.
- To change the physical size of an image without affecting its resolution, uncheck the "Resample" option and adjust the width or height values.
- To resample an image, which means to change its resolution and physical size, check the "Resample" option and adjust the width, height, or resolution values. Keep in mind that increasing

the size of an image beyond its original size can result in a loss of quality and detail.

- When preparing images for print, it is recommended to use a resolution of at least 300 PPI to ensure high-quality output. For digital media, such as web or social media, a lower resolution of 72 PPI or 96 PPI may be sufficient.

By understanding image resolution and size and how to adjust them in Photoshop, you can optimize your images for different purposes and achieve the best possible results.

UNDERSTANDING COLOR MODES

Color mode refers to the color model used to display and print an image. Photoshop supports various color modes, including RGB, CMYK, Grayscale, Lab, and more. Each color mode has its unique properties and uses.

Here is a basic procedure for changing the color mode in Photoshop:

1. Open the image you want to change the color mode for in Photoshop.
2. Go to the Image menu and choose Mode.

3. Select the color mode you want to change the image to. For example, if you're going to change an RGB image to CMYK, select CMYK Color.
4. A dialog box will appear, asking you to confirm the color mode change. Click OK.
5. If you are converting to a color mode with a smaller gamut (range of colors) than the original color mode, you may be prompted with another dialog box asking if you want to flatten the layers. Click OK to continue.
6. If necessary, make any adjustments to the image to account for the differences in color between the two color modes.
7. Save the image by going to File > Save As and choosing a file format and location.

It's important to note that changing the color mode of an image can affect its appearance and quality, especially when converting from RGB to CMYK. It's recommended to work in the appropriate color mode for the image's intended use to ensure the best results.

COLOR CORRECTION

Color correction is the process of adjusting the colors in an image to make them more accurate, consistent, or aesthetically pleasing. Here's a basic procedure for performing color correction in Photoshop:

1. Open the image you want to correct in Photoshop.
2. Make sure the Layers panel is open by going to Window > Layers. If your image has a Background layer, double-click on it to convert it to a regular layer.
3. Create a new adjustment layer by clicking on the "Create new fill or adjustment layer" button at the bottom of the Layers panel, as shown previously, and choose one of the following options:

- Brightness/Contrast: This adjustment lets you adjust the overall brightness and contrast of the image.
- Levels: This adjustment lets you adjust the brightness and contrast of the image using the black, white, and gray points.
- Curves: This adjustment lets you adjust the brightness and contrast of the image using a graph with control points.
- Color Balance: This adjustment lets you adjust the balance between the colors in the image.

- Hue/Saturation: This adjustment lets you adjust the hue, saturation, and lightness of the colors in the image.

4. Use the adjustment layer's controls to make the necessary color corrections. You can adjust the sliders or enter numerical values to fine-tune the adjustments.
5. If you want to apply the color correction to a specific part of the image, you can use a layer mask to hide or reveal the adjustment. Click on the layer mask icon at the bottom of the adjustment layer, and use a brush tool to paint on the mask with black or white to hide or reveal parts of the adjustment.
6. If you are satisfied with the color correction, you can save the image by going to File > Save As and choosing a file format and location.

Color correction can be a complex and subjective process, and the specific techniques and tools you use will depend on the nature and requirements of the image. However, by following these basic steps, you can start to improve the colors of your images in Photoshop.

RETOUCHING AND REPAIRING IMAGES

Retouching and repairing images involves a range of techniques that are used to enhance or correct imperfections in an image. Here's a basic procedure for retouching and repairing images in Photoshop:

1. Open the image you want to retouch or repair in Photoshop.
2. Assess the image and determine what needs to be fixed or enhanced. Common issues include blemishes, scratches, dust, and other imperfections.
3. Choose the appropriate tool for the job. For example, if you want to remove a blemish, use the spot healing brush tool.
4. Adjust the settings of the tool as needed. For example, you may need to adjust the brush's size, hardness, or opacity to achieve the desired effect.
5. Apply the tool to the area of the image that needs to be fixed or enhanced. Be careful not to overdo it or create an unnatural-looking result.
6. Repeat the process as needed for other areas of the image.
7. Use adjustment layers or other techniques to enhance the color, brightness, contrast, or other aspects of the image if needed.

8. Save the image by going to File > Save As and choosing a file format and location.

It's important to note that retouching and repairing images can be time-consuming, especially for more complex issues. However, you can achieve a more polished and professional result by using these basic techniques and taking the time to assess and work on each area of the image carefully.

CROPPING IMAGES

Cropping allows you to adjust the size and dimensions of your image, remove unwanted parts, or change the aspect ratio.

Here's an overview of how to crop images in Photoshop:

Cropping:

1. Open the image you want to crop in Photoshop.
2. Select the Crop tool from the toolbar or press the "C" key.
3. Drag the Crop tool over the area you want to keep in the image. You can adjust the size and shape of the crop by dragging the handles on the edges of the selection.

4. Press Enter/Return or click the checkmark icon in the Options bar to apply the crop.
5. Save your cropped image by going to File > Save As and choosing a file format and location.

Using this simple technique, you can crop your images to fit your needs and create the perfect composition.

SHARPENING AND BLURRING IMAGES

Sharpening and blurring are common image editing techniques used in Photoshop to enhance or soften the image. Here's an overview of how to sharpen and blur images in Photoshop:

Sharpening:

1. Open the image you want to sharpen in Photoshop.
2. Duplicate the layer by going to Layer > Duplicate Layer or by pressing the keyboard shortcut Ctrl+J (Windows) or Command+J (Mac). This is a good practice to avoid damaging the original image.
3. Select the duplicated layer in the Layers panel.
4. Go to Filter > Sharpen > Unsharp Mask to open the Unsharp Mask dialog box.

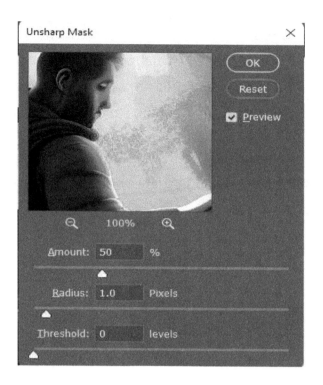

5. Adjust the Amount, Radius, and Threshold sliders until you achieve the desired level of sharpening. Preview the effect by checking the "Preview" checkbox.

6. Click OK to apply the sharpening effect.

7. If necessary, adjust the layer opacity or layer blend mode to fine-tune the effect.

8. Save your sharpened image by going to File > Save As and choosing a file format and location.

Blurring:

1. Open the image you want to blur in Photoshop.
2. Duplicate the layer by going to Layer > Duplicate Layer or by pressing the keyboard shortcut Ctrl+J (Windows) or Command+J (Mac). This is a good practice to avoid damaging the original image.
3. Select the duplicated layer in the Layers panel.
4. Go to Filter > Blur and choose the type of blur you want to apply. Gaussian Blur is a good choice for most images.
5. Adjust the Radius slider until you achieve the desired level of blur. Preview the effect by checking the "Preview" checkbox.

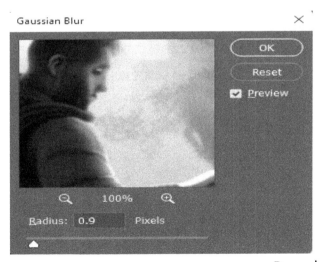

6. Click OK to apply the blur effect.
7. If necessary, adjust the layer opacity or layer blend mode to fine-tune the effect.
8. Save your blurred image by going to File > Save As and choosing a file format and location.

By using these simple techniques, you can sharpen or blur your images to make them more visually appealing or to convey a specific mood or feeling.

ADDING TEXT AND GRAPHICS

Adding text and graphics to an image in Photoshop is a common task for designers and photographers. Here's a general procedure to follow when adding text and graphics to an image in Photoshop:

1. Open the image in Photoshop.
2. Select the Text tool from the toolbar on the left-hand side of the screen.
3. Click on the image where you want to add text and start typing. You can choose the font, size, and color of the text from the options at the top of the screen.
4. To add graphics, go to File > Place Embedded or Place Linked and choose the image you want to

add. You can also drag and drop the image directly onto the canvas.

5. Position and resize the graphics as needed using the Transform tool (Ctrl+T or Command+T).
6. Adjust the opacity and blend mode of the graphics layer if necessary to blend it with the background image.
7. Apply layer styles or effects to the text and graphics layer to make them stand out or blend with the image.
8. Save your edited image by going to File > Save As and choosing a file format and location.

By following these simple steps, you can add text and graphics to your images in Photoshop to create compelling designs and visually exciting compositions.

REMOVING THE BACKGROUND OF AN IMAGE

Removing the background of an image can be challenging, but Photoshop offers several tools and techniques to accomplish this. Here's a general procedure to follow when removing the background of an image in Photoshop:

1. Open the image in Photoshop.

2. Duplicate the background layer by right-clicking on the layer and selecting Duplicate Layer. This is a good practice to avoid damaging the original image.
3. Choose the selection tool you want to use to select the background. The Magic Wand or Quick Selection tools are good options for selecting simple backgrounds, while the Pen tool is better suited for more complex backgrounds.
4. Adjust the size of the tool selected, if necessary, at the Options bar
5. Select the background by clicking and dragging over it with your selected tool. If necessary, refine your selection using the options in the toolbar.
6. Invert the selection by going to Select > Inverse or using the keyboard shortcut Ctrl+Shift+I (Command+Shift+I on a Mac).
7. Delete the selected area by pressing the Delete key or using the keyboard shortcut Ctrl+X (Command+X on a Mac).
8. Fine-tune the edges of the image by using the Refine Edge tool or manually adjusting the selection using the eraser tool.
9. Save your edited image by going to File > Save As and choosing a file format and location.

By following these general steps, you can remove the background of an image in Photoshop and create transparent or new background layers. It may take some practice to master the techniques involved, but with time and patience, you can achieve great results.

PART 7 → FILE FORMATS AND OUTPUT

When you're done creating your image in Photoshop, it's essential to save it in the proper file format to ensure that it looks its best and can be used for its intended purpose.

UNDERSTANDING FILE FORMATS

Understanding file formats is crucial when creating images for web and print. Here are some commonly used file formats and their best uses:

For web:

1. JPEG: This format is ideal for photographs and images with many colors. It compresses the file size, which makes it an excellent format for web use.

2. PNG: This format is excellent for images with transparent backgrounds or images with fewer colors. It's also a good choice for web use, as it can preserve image quality while still having a relatively small file size.

3. GIF: This format is ideal for simple graphics, such as logos or icons, that need to be animated. It supports transparency and animation, making it an excellent choice for web use.

For print:

1. TIFF: This format is best for images that need to be printed at high resolutions, such as photos or illustrations. It preserves image quality and can store multiple layers.
2. PSD: This is Photoshop's native file format, which preserves all of the layers, masks, and other information you've added to your image. This is a great format to use if you need to edit the image later or if you want to make sure that the printed image looks exactly as you intended.
3. PDF: This format is excellent for print layouts, including text and images, such as brochures or flyers. It can be easily printed and preserve the original document's layout and formatting.

Understanding the best file format for web and print can ensure that your images look their best and can be used for their intended purpose. It's important to consider factors such as image quality, file size, and transparency when choosing a file format for your project.

EXPORTING PHOTOSHOP FILES

Exporting files from Adobe Photoshop can be done using the following steps:

1. Open your image or design in Photoshop and make any necessary edits.
2. Go to File > Export > Export As or File > Export > Save for Web (Legacy), depending on your desired format and settings.
3. In the "Export" or "Save for Web" dialog box, choose the file format you want to export to (such as JPEG, PNG, GIF, or PDF).

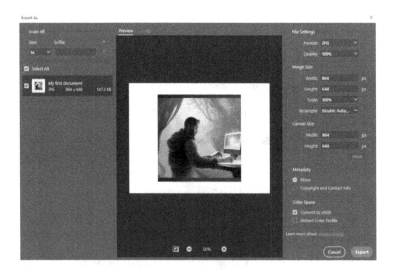

4. Adjust any export settings as needed, such as image quality, resolution, compression, or color mode.

5. Preview your export settings and make any necessary adjustments.
6. Click "Export" or "Save".
7. Choose a destination folder and filename for your exported file.
8. Click "Save" to save your file to your computer.

Depending on the file format and settings you choose, additional options may be available in the export dialog box, such as transparency, layers, compression, or optimization. Make sure to choose the appropriate format and settings for your intended use, whether for web or print, and save your file in a high-quality format that preserves your design and image integrity.

PRINTING IMAGES

Printing images from Adobe Photoshop involves the following steps:

1. Open your image in Photoshop and make any necessary adjustments or edits.
2. Go to File > Print or use the shortcut Ctrl + P (Windows) or Cmd + P (Mac).

3. In the Print dialog box, choose the printer you want to use and any other settings such as paper size, orientation, and print quality.

4. Preview your print settings and make any necessary adjustments.
5. Set up any additional options such as color management, scaling, or positioning of the image on the paper.
6. Load your paper into the printer and click "Print" to start the printing process.

Make sure to choose the appropriate paper type, size, and quality settings to ensure the best results for your printed image. It's also a good idea to preview your print settings and make any necessary adjustments before printing to avoid wasting paper and ink. Finally, it's recommended to calibrate your monitor and printer to ensure that the colors on your screen match those on your printed image.

EXPORTING PHOTOSHOP FILES FOR OTHER SOFTWARE

When exporting Photoshop files for other software, there are a few things to keep in mind:

1. File format: Choose the appropriate file format based on the software requirements you're exporting to. Common formats include PSD, TIFF, JPEG, and PNG.
2. Layers: Depending on the software you're exporting to, you may need to merge or flatten your layers before exporting. This is especially true if the software does not support layers or if you want to preserve the appearance of your layers as a single image.
3. Resolution: Consider the file's resolution and the software requirements you're exporting to. For example, if you're exporting to a web application, use a lower resolution to reduce file size and loading times. On the other hand, if you're exporting to a high-quality print application, use a

higher resolution to ensure the best possible print quality.

4. Color space: Consider the color space of your file and the requirements of the software you're exporting to. For example, if you're exporting to a web application, use the sRGB color space, which is commonly used for web graphics. If you're exporting to a print application, use the CMYK color space, which is commonly used for print graphics.

5. File size: Consider the file size of your exported file and the requirements of the software you're exporting to. For example, some software may have file size limits, so you may need to adjust the resolution, compression, or other settings to reduce the file size.

By considering these factors, you can ensure that your Photoshop files are properly exported for use in other software.

SHARING PHOTOSHOP FILES

When it comes to sharing files created in Photoshop, there are several options available depending on your needs:

1. Photoshop software: You can share files in Photoshop by going to File > Share. This allows you to share your files through email, Bluetooth, WIFI, etc.
2. Email: You can attach the Photoshop file to an email and send it to the recipient.
3. Cloud storage: You can use cloud storage services such as Dropbox, Google Drive, or OneDrive to upload and share the file. This allows the recipient to access the file from anywhere with an internet connection.
4. File sharing platforms: There are several online platforms available such as WeTransfer, Send Anywhere, or Hightail, that allows you to upload and share large files.
5. Social media: You can also share your Photoshop files on social media platforms such as Instagram, Facebook, or Twitter. However, remember that these platforms may compress the file and reduce its quality.
6. FTP: If you have access to an FTP server, you can upload the file to the server and provide the recipient with access to the file.

When sharing files, it's important to consider the file size and the recipient's ability to open and view it. If the recipient can't access Photoshop, consider exporting the file in a different format, such as JPEG or PNG.

PART 8 → ADVANCED TECHNIQUES AND TIPS

These techniques can help you create more complex and unique designs, work more efficiently, and take your skills to the next level.

USING ACTIONS AND BATCH PROCESSING

Actions and Batch processing are powerful tools in Photoshop that can save you time and improve your workflow. Actions are recordings of a series of steps that you can apply to multiple images to automate repetitive tasks. Batch processing allows you to apply these actions to a large number of images at once, which is particularly useful when working with a large number of files. These tools can be used to perform a wide range of tasks, from simple image adjustments to complex tasks such as creating HDR images or stitching panoramas.

Here are the general steps to use Actions and Batch processing in Photoshop:

1. Create an Action: Open an image and go to the Actions panel (Window > Actions). Click the

"Create new action" button and give it a name. Start recording the action by clicking the "Record" button.

2. Perform the desired steps: Perform the desired steps on the image. This can include basic adjustments like resizing or cropping or more complex actions like applying filters, adjusting colors, or adding layers.

3. Stop recording the action: When you have finished performing the steps, stop recording the action by clicking the "Stop" button in the Actions panel.

4. Apply the action: With the action saved, you can now apply it to other images. To do this, go to File > Automate > Batch. Select the action you want to apply from the "Set" dropdown list, choose the source folder where your images are located, and set the destination folder where you want the processed images to be saved.

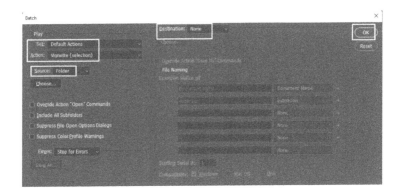

5. Run the batch: Click "OK" to run the batch. Photoshop will process all of the images in the source folder using the specified action and save the processed files to the destination folder.

Using Actions and Batch processing in Photoshop can save you a lot of time and help streamline your workflow. With a bit of practice and experimentation, you can create customized actions to automate tasks and batch process large numbers of images quickly and easily.

WORKING WITH 3D OBJECTS

Working with 3D objects in Photoshop allows you to create and manipulate 3D models, textures, and lighting to produce realistic-looking objects or scenes. This involves importing 3D models, applying textures, adding materials, and using different lighting techniques to create realistic 3D effects. You can also use 3D layers to create 3D text, logos, or other objects that can be easily edited and manipulated. Advanced techniques include using 3D features such as Depth Maps and Mesh from Grayscale to create custom 3D objects, and using the Vanishing Point feature to create realistic 3D scenes from 2D images.

Here are the general procedures for working with 3D objects in Photoshop:

1. Import a 3D model: Go to "3D" menu and choose "New 3D from File" to import a 3D model in a supported format (such as OBJ or Collada).
2. Apply textures and materials: Use the "3D Materials" panel to apply textures and materials to the 3D model.
3. Position and rotate the 3D object: Use the "3D Move" tool to position and rotate the 3D object in the workspace.

4. Adjust lighting and shadows: Use the "3D Lighting" panel to adjust lighting and shadows to create a realistic effect.
5. Customize the 3D object: Use the various 3D features such as Depth Maps and Mesh from Grayscale to create custom 3D objects.
6. Add 3D text or logos: Use the 3D layers to create 3D text, logos, or other objects that can be easily edited and manipulated.
7. Use the Vanishing Point feature: Use the Vanishing Point feature to create realistic 3D scenes from 2D images.
8. Export or save the 3D object: Use the "Export 3D Layer" command to save the 3D object in a format that can be used in other applications or save the file as a PSD file for future editing.

WORKING WITH VIDEO

Working with video in Photoshop involves various techniques and procedures, such as importing video files, trimming and splitting clips, adding effects and transitions, and exporting the final video. It also includes working with timelines, keyframes, and audio tracks, and integrating video with other Photoshop projects.

Here is a general procedure for working with video in Photoshop:

1. Import the video file: Go to File > Import > Video Frames to Layers to import a video file as a series of still images, or go to File > Open Video to open the video file directly.
2. Edit the video: Use the timeline panel to trim, split, and reorder the video clips as needed. You can also add effects and transitions, adjust the color and lighting, and use keyframes to create animations and movements.
3. Add audio: If your video includes audio, you can edit it directly in the timeline panel or use the audio timeline panel to adjust the volume, add effects, and synchronize it with the video.
4. Export the video: Once you have finished editing your video, go to File > Export > Render Video to export the final video in a suitable format and quality. You can choose from various options, such as resolution, frame rate, and compression settings.
5. Integration with other projects: You can also integrate your video with other Photoshop

projects, such as creating a video slideshow or incorporating video into a larger design project.

Note that the specific steps and tools used may vary depending on the version of Photoshop and the complexity of the video project. It is also recommended to have a basic understanding of video editing concepts and terminology before working with video in Photoshop.

CREATING ANIMATIONS

Creating animations in Photoshop is a fun and creative process that can be used for various purposes, from creating GIFs to adding motion to your designs. Here's a general procedure to follow when creating animations in Photoshop:

1. Create a new document in Photoshop with the desired dimensions and resolution.
2. Create a new layer for each frame of your animation.
3. Add content to each layer to create the desired animation. This can include text, images, or other design elements.

4. Open the Timeline panel by going to Window > Timeline.

5. In the Timeline panel, click on "Create Video Timeline".

6. Adjust the duration for each frame by dragging the edge.

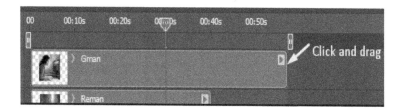

7. Arrange the frame as you want them to appear by dragging them.

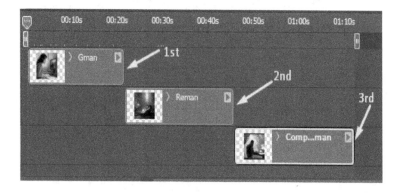

8. Click the options button in the Timeline panel and click Convert Frames > Convert to Frame Animation.

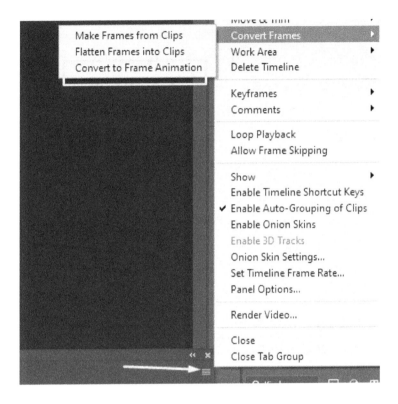

9. Set the duration for each frame by clicking on the dropdown menu next to each layer in the Timeline panel and selecting the desired time.
10. Preview your animation by clicking on the Play button in the Timeline panel.
11. If desired, you can add additional animation effects, such as transitions or special effects, using the Animation panel.

12.Save your animation by going to File > Export > Save for Web (Legacy) and choosing a file format and location.

By following these general steps, you can create Photoshop animations tailored to your needs and preferences. Keep in mind that the process of creating animations can be time-consuming, but the result is well worth the effort.

USING PLUGINS AND EXTENSIONS

Plugins and extensions are additional software tools that can be installed in Adobe Photoshop to extend its functionality. To use plugins and extensions, you can follow these general steps:

1. Install the plugin or extension: Download and install the plugin or extension from the developer's website or through the Adobe Creative Cloud Marketplace.
2. Open Photoshop: Launch Photoshop and ensure that the plugin or extension is installed and activated.
3. Locate the plugin or extension: Depending on the plugin or extension, it may be located in different

places in the Photoshop interface. For example, some plugins may be located under the Filters menu, while others may have a dedicated panel in the interface.

4. Use the plugin or extension: Follow the instructions provided by the plugin or extension to use its features. Some plugins may have settings and parameters that you can adjust to customize the effect or output.

5. Save or export your work: After using the plugin or extension, you can save or export your work in the desired format or file type.

It's important to note that not all plugins and extensions are compatible with all versions of Photoshop, so be sure to check the compatibility requirements before installing. Additionally, some plugins and extensions may be free, while others may require a purchase or subscription.

PART 9 → CONCLUSION

In conclusion, Adobe Photoshop is a powerful and versatile tool that can be used for a wide range of image editing tasks. With its vast array of features and tools, users can create stunning visuals and manipulate images in various ways. From basic tasks such as creating and saving documents to more advanced techniques such as working with 3D objects and video, there is a lot to explore and learn in Photoshop. With practice and experimentation, users can unlock the full potential of this powerful software and take their creativity to the next level.

TIPS FOR IMPROVING YOUR PHOTOSHOP SKILLS

Here are some tips for improving your Photoshop skills:

1. Practice regularly: The more you use Photoshop, the better you will become at it. Try to make it a habit to practice and experiment with new techniques and tools.
2. Take online courses: There are many online courses and tutorials available that can help you

learn new skills and techniques in Photoshop. Take advantage of these resources to enhance your skills.

3. Join online communities: Joining online communities of Photoshop users can provide you with a platform to learn from others, ask questions, and share your work.

4. Experiment with new techniques: Be bold and try out new techniques and tools in Photoshop. Experimenting can help you discover new ways of doing things and expand your skill set.

5. Keep up with updates: Photoshop is constantly evolving, and it's important to stay up-to-date with the latest updates and features to take full advantage of the software's capabilities.

6. Take breaks: It's easy to get burned out when working on a project for too long. Take regular breaks to recharge your creative energy and return to your work with a fresh perspective.

7. Stay organized: Keeping your files and layers organized can save you a lot of time and frustration in the long run. Develop a system for naming and grouping your layers and files to keep everything organized and easy to find.

RESOURCES FOR FURTHER LEARNING

There are several resources available for further learning and improving your Photoshop skills. Some of them include:

1. Adobe Photoshop Help: This is the official help center for Adobe Photoshop. It offers tutorials, user guides, and troubleshooting information.
2. YouTube: There are many tutorials available on YouTube that can help you improve your Photoshop skills.
3. Photoshop forums: Joining Photoshop forums like Adobe Support Community and Photoshop Gurus can help you learn from other Photoshop users and experts.

By utilizing these resources, you can continue to improve your Photoshop skills and create even more impressive designs and artworks.

EXERCISES

Here are a few exercises for beginners to practice on Adobe Photoshop:

1. Basic photo editing: Choose a photo and practice adjusting its brightness, contrast, and color balance. Try different adjustment tools to see how they affect the photo.
2. Creating a collage: Gather a few images and create a collage by arranging and resizing them on a blank canvas. Add some text or shapes to make it more interesting.
3. Removing an object: Choose an image and practice removing an unwanted object using the Clone Stamp or Healing Brush tool. Make sure to blend the removed area with the rest of the image.
4. Creating a simple logo: Create a logo using basic shapes and text tools. Experiment with different fonts and colors to create a unique design.
5. Designing a social media graphic: Choose a social media platform and create a graphic using the appropriate dimensions. Add some text and images to make it visually appealing.

These exercises will help you get familiar with Adobe Photoshop and its tools.

OTHER BOOKS

Thank you for your purchase! If you enjoyed this book, check out our other titles. We have a great selection of books on various topics that interest you. Happy reading!

Dear Reader, if you enjoyed reading my book, I would be very grateful if you could take a few moments to leave a review. Your feedback means a lot to me and will help others discover the book. Thank you so much for your support!